OF THE UPPER JURASSIC

DAVID & OLIVER WEST

FIREFLY BOOKS

A FIREFLY BOOK

Published by Firefly Books Ltd. 2016

First printing

Publisher Cataloging-in-Publication Data (U.S.)

Names: West, David, 1956-, author.
Title: Dinosaurs of the Upper Jurassic : 25 dinosaurs / David West.
Description: Richmond Hill, Ontario, Canada : Firefly Books, 2016. | Series: Dinosaurs. | Includes index. | Summary: "An illustrated guide of 25 of the best-known dinosaurs of the period, providing up-to-date information with highly detailed computer generated artwork. Illustrated introductory spreads provide background information on the time periods in which the dinosaurs lived" -- Provided by publisher.
Identifiers: ISBN 978-1-77085-839-8 (paperback) | 978-1-77085-840-4 (hardcover)
Subjects: LCSH: Dinosaurs – Juvenile literature.
Classification: LCC QE861.5W478 |DDC 567.9 – dc23

Library and Archives Canada Cataloguing in Publication

West, David, 1956-, author
        Dinosaurs of the upper Jurassic : 25 dinos... / David West.
(Dinosaurs)
Includes index.
ISBN 978-1-77085-840-4 (hardback).--ISBN 978-1-77085-839-8 (paperback)
        1. Dinosaurs--Juvenile literature. 2. Paleontology--Jurassic--Juvenile literature. I. Title.
QE861.5.W4694 2016   j567.9   C2016-902146-7

Published in the United States by
Firefly Books (U.S.) Inc.
P.O. Box 1338, Ellicott Station
Buffalo, New York 14205

Published in Canada by
Firefly Books Ltd.
50 Staples Avenue, Unit 1
Richmond Hill, Ontario L4B 0A7

Printed in China

Text by David and Oliver West
Illustrations by David West

Produced by David West
Children's Books,
6 Princeton Court, 55 Felsham
Road, London SW15 1AZ

CONTENTS

THE UPPER JURASSIC

The Upper Jurassic lasted from 164 to 145 million years ago. The land area was broken into two land masses called Laurasia in the north and Gondwana in the south. New seas and oceans developed as the two masses spread apart. Sea levels were high and became higher during the Upper Cretaceous. The Laurasian landmass was broken up by the rising sea and islands formed in what is today Europe.

A warm, humid climate allowed lush jungles to cover much of the landscape. Conifers, cycads, ginkgo plants and tree ferns dominated with smaller ferns making up much of the undergrowth.

This time was a golden age for the large herbivorous dinosaurs known as the **sauropods** and spiky **stegosaurs**. They were preyed upon by big predators such as *Megalosaurus*, *Torvosaurus* (see page 29) and *Allosaurus* (see page 6). The first bird-like animals, such as *Archaeopteryx* (see page 8), evolved while the air was ruled by the **pterosaurs**.

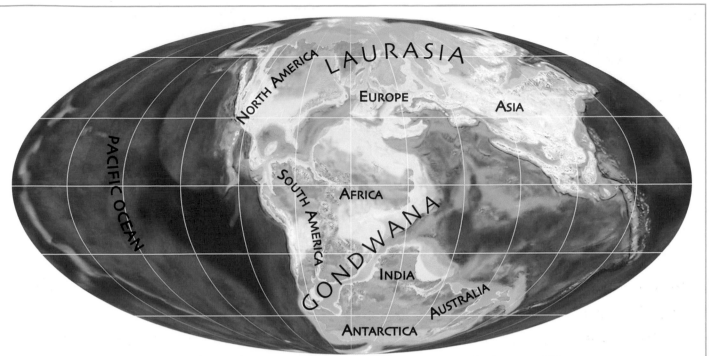

This map shows the Earth at the time of the Upper Jurassic period 150 million years ago. Below, a scene from the European Jurassic 150 million years ago shows an Archaeopteryx (1) glide past a pair of Europasauruses (2). A Miragaia (3) ambles along the shore as a group of Compsognathuses (4) chase two Juravenators (5). Behind, pterosaurs (6) search for fish.

ALLOSAURUS

Allosaurus, meaning "strange lizard," was a large **theropod**. It had two bony horns that protruded above its eyes and may have protected them when it fought. It might have hunted in packs, preying on *Stegosaurus* (see page 27) and large **sauropods** such as *Diplodocus* (see page 17). *Allosaurus* was probably hunted by other predators such as *Torvosaurus* (see page 29) that lived in the same dry flood plains where it preferred to hunt.

Allosaurus lived **153–135 million years ago**. Fossil remains have been found in Portugal, Europe, and the United States, North America. It averaged 28 feet (8.5 m) in length and weighed around 2.5 tons (2.3 tonnes).

APATOSAURUS

The name *Apatosaurus* means "deceptive lizard." It was a large, herbivorous **sauropod** that lived in what is now North America. *Apatosaurus* had a long, horizontal neck that allowed the dinosaur to reach into thickly wooded or swampy areas to feed. It had peg-like teeth that stripped leaves from branches, which it would then swallow without chewing. To help digestion *Apatosaurus* swallowed stones to grind down the plant material in its stomach.

Apatosaurus lived between **154–145 million years ago**. Fossil remains have been found all over the United States, North America. It grew to an average length of 82 feet (25 m) and weighed about 18.7 tons (17 tonnes.)

ARCHAEOPTERYX

Archaeopteryx, meaning "ancient wing," was a bird-like dinosaur. It has been classed as a member of the bird family and its fossils are a record of the evolutionary link between dinosaurs and birds. It had wings and a long tail. On each wing it had a clawed hand that it could use to climb trees or grasp prey. Its feathers were not as rigid as modern birds', but they had the central shaft that would have enabled it to glide. *Archaeopteryx* shared many traits with **dromaeosaurs** and **troodons,** such as their jaws with sharp teeth, three fingers with claws — and its long bony tail, which was probably more a counterbalance device than an aid to flight.

Archaeopteryx lived **150 million years ago**. Fossil remains have been found in Germany, Europe. It grew to about 1 foot (30.5 cm) long, with a wingspan of 1.5 feet (45.7 cm), and weighed up to 2 pounds (0.9 kg).

BRACHIOSAURUS

This **sauropod** —*Brachiosaurus*— was one of the largest animals to have walked the Earth. Its name means "arm lizard" because its front legs (arms) were longer than its back legs. Its height allowed it to crop vegetation as high as 30 feet (9 m) from the ground. Its diet consisted of the leaves of ginkgoes, conifers, tree ferns and large cycads. It would munch on an estimated 441–882 pounds (200–400 kg) of plant matter every day.

Brachiosaurus lived **155–140 million years ago**. Fossil remains have been found in Algeria and Tanzania, Africa; Portugal, Europe; and the United States, North America. It grew to 82 feet (25 m) long and weighed 77 tons (70 tonnes).

BRACHYTRACHELOPAN

Brachytrachelopan means "short-necked Pan." Pan was a shepherd god, and the dinosaur was given this name because its fossils were found by a shepherd looking for his lost sheep! *Brachytrachelopan* was a herbivorous dinosaur that evolved with a shorter neck than is usual for a **sauropod** because it had adapted to grazing on low- to medium-height vegetation. This meant it did not compete for the same food as the long-necked **sauropods** it coexisted with.

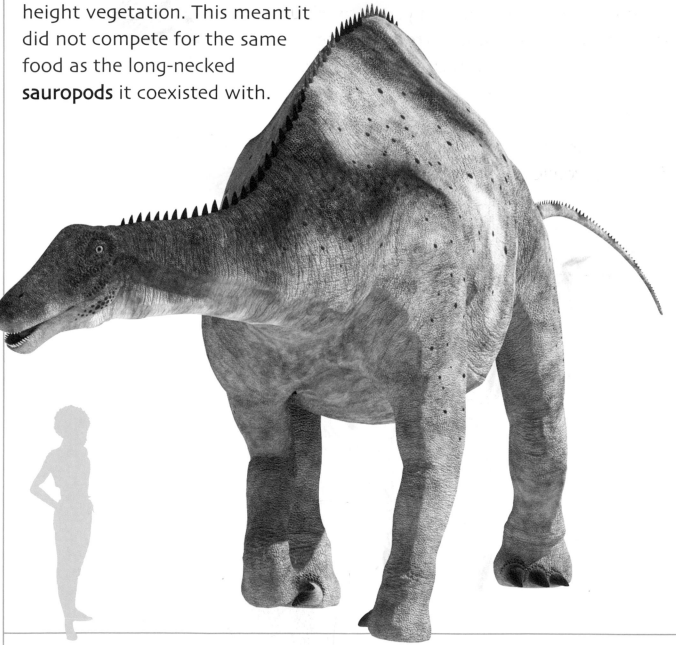

Brachytrachelopan lived about **150 million years ago**. Fossil remains were found in Argentina, South America. It grew to 33 feet (10 m) long and weighed between 5 and 10 tons (4.5–9 tonnes).

CAMARASAURUS

Camarasaurus was a very large herbivorous **sauropod** named after the hollow chambers found in its vertebrae. Its name means "chamber lizard." *Camarasaurus* is thought to have laid its eggs in a line near wooded areas with undergrowth, but it did not look after them. When the eggs hatched the young headed for the cover of the undergrowth. Here they stayed until they grew large enough to join a herd on the open plains. There is fossil evidence of *Camarasauruses* living in herds, which may have provided safety for the juveniles.

Camarasaurus lived between **150–140 million years ago**. Fossil remains were found in the United States, North America. It could grow up to 75 feet (23 m) long and weighed about 52 tons (47 tonnes).

CAMPTOSAURUS

Camptosaurus means "bent lizard." It was a herbivorous **ornithopod** that walked on two legs but grazed on all fours. Its rear legs were longer and more powerful than its forelimbs, and could carry the dinosaur at speeds of up to 15 mph (24 km/h). It had a triangular skull that ended in a beak, but it also had hundreds of teeth. Fossils show that these teeth were often very worn down, so *Camptosaurus* would have chewed its food well. It may also have preferred to eat tougher vegetation that other dinosaurs avoided.

Camptosaurus lived **150 million years ago**. Fossil remains have been found in the Western United States, North America. It grew up to 23 feet (7 m) long and weighed about 0.88 tons (0.8 tonnes).

CERATOSAURUS

Ceratosaurus, meaning "horned lizard," was named after its horns. It was a carnivorous **theropod**, with small arms and four fingers instead of the usual three. Its body and tail were flexible, suggesting it may have been a good swimmer and probably hunted fish and crocodiles. It was smaller than other **theropods** of the time such as *Torvosaurus* (see page 29) and *Allosaurus* (see page 6).

Ceratosaurus lived about **150 million years ago**. Fossil remains were found in Utah in the United States, North America. It could grow to 18 to 20 feet (5.4–7.6 m) long and could weigh about 0.5 to 1 ton (0.45–0.9 tonnes).

COELURUS

Coelurus means "hollow tail" and was named after the hollow vertebrae in its tail. Many of *Coelurus'* bones had hollow pockets, especially in the neck, making it one of the lightest dinosaurs. *Coelurus* was a small **theropod** similar in shape and size to *Ornitholestes* (see page 25). It had an elongated neck and long legs, perfect for running. Its lightness made it incredibly agile and it was perhaps one of the fastest dinosaurs for its size.

Coelurus lived **150 million years ago**. Its fossil remains were found in Wyoming in the United States. It could grow up to 6.6 feet (2 m) long and weighed approximately 28.7 to 44 pounds (13–20 kg.)

COMPSOGNATHUS

Compsognathus was a small, delicate **theropod** dinosaur that probably fed on small insects and lizards. Its name means "delicate jaw." It lived on islands on the edge of the Tethys Ocean. No other dinosaur fossils have been found alongside these little creatures, which suggests that they were the top land predators of their environment.

Compsognathus lived **150 million years ago**. Fossil remains have been found in France and Germany, Europe. It grew to around 3.3 feet (1 m) long and weighed between 1.8 and 7.7 pounds (0.8–3.5 kg).

DICRAEOSAURUS

Dicraeosaurus, meaning "forked lizard," is named after the forked spines that emerge from its neck and back in two parallel rows. It was a small **sauropod** with a short neck. It browsed on vegetation at ground level and up to a height of about 9.8 feet (3 m). It is thought these spines may have been a defense against tall **theropods** biting down onto its back or neck.

Dicraeosaurus lived between **150–135 million years ago**. Fossil remains have been found in Tanzania, Africa. It grew up to 41 feet (12 m) long and weighed 6 tons (5.4 tonnes).

DIPLODOCUS

Diplodocus was a large plant-eating **sauropod** with a very long tail that it may have used like a whip to drive predators away. The middle part of the tail had "double beams," oddly shaped bones on the underside, which gave *Diplodocus* its name. *Diplodocus* had strange peg-like teeth that it used to strip leaves from the branches of trees. *Diplodocus'* teeth were continually replaced throughout its life. Each tooth socket had as many as five replacement teeth developing, ready to replace the worn-down one.

Diplodocus lived **155–145 million years ago**. Fossil remains have been found in the United States, North America. It grew to around 98.4 feet (30 m) long and weighed up to 17.6 tons (16 tonnes).

EUROPASAURUS

Europasaurus means "Europe lizard." It was a small **sauropod**, similar to *Brachiosaurus* (see page 9), with long front legs, short hind legs and a sloping back. It lived on small islands when most of Europe was under water. The limited food supply on these islands could not support large dinosaurs, so these **sauropods** evolved into smaller animals. This is known as island dwarfism.

Europasaurus lived **154–151 million years ago**. Its fossil remains have been found in Germany, Europe. It grew to 20 feet (6.1 m) long and weighed in excess of 0.55 tons (0.5 tonnes).

GARGOYLEOSAURUS

Gargoyleosaurus means "gargoyle lizard," after the almost stone-like protective armor that covered it. It was one of the earliest-known **ankylosaurs**, and shared many characteristics with the group, including the heavy armor plating down its back. It also had spikes running down each side of its body. **Ankylosaurs** were herbivores and used their beaks to chomp off vegetation from low-lying plants. Unlike other **ankylosaurs**, *Gargoyleosaurus* had teeth on both the upper and lower jaws that allowed it to chew food more effectively.

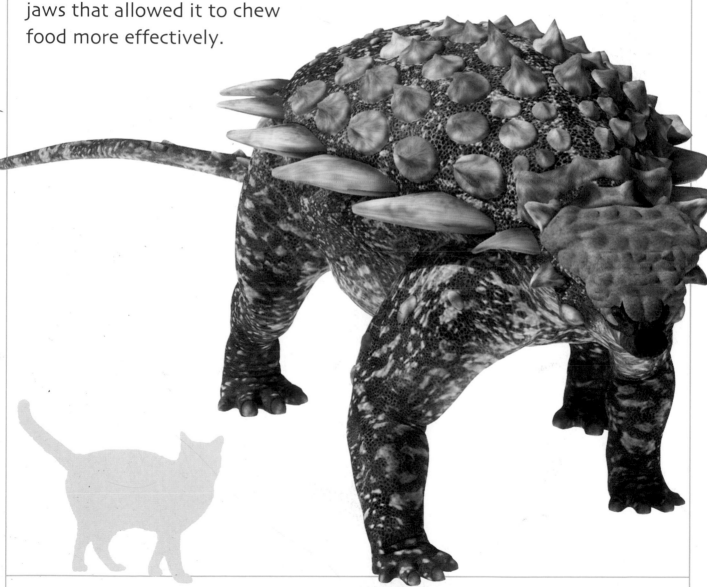

Gargoyleosaurus lived between **155–144 million years ago**. Fossil remains have been found in the United States, North America. It grew to a length of 9 to 13 feet (2.7–4 m) and a weight of around 1.1 tons (1 tonne).

GIGANTSPINOSAURUS

Gigantspinosaurus is named after the giant spikes on its shoulder. Its name means "giant-spined lizard." It was one of the earliest and smallest **stegosaurs**. Although its back plates were much smaller than those on *Stegosaurus* (see page 27), its huge, scythe-like shoulder spines would have given it protection from predators. It also had two pairs of spikes at the end if its tail.

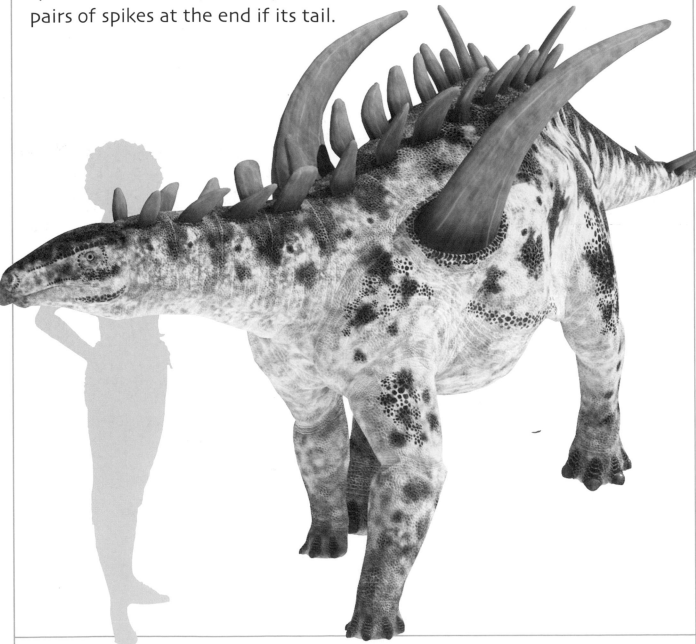

Gigantspinosaurus lived about **160 million years ago**. Fossil remains were found in the Sichuan province in China, Asia. It grew to about 13 feet (4 m) long and weighed around 1,500 pounds (680 kg).

JURAVENATOR

Juravenator was a small bipedal predator that hunted small reptiles and insects. It was a **theropod** dinosaur and its name means "hunter from Jura," after where its fossils were found. *Juravenator* was similar to *Compsognathus* (see page 15), and lived around the same time. They were probably the top predators of their island habitat.

Juravenator lived **154–151 million years ago**. Fossil remains have been found in Germany, Europe. It grew to around 2 feet (0.8 m) long and weighed less than 2.2 pounds (1 kg).

KENTROSAURUS

Kentrosaurus belonged to the **stegosaur** family of plant-eating dinosaurs. It was smaller than *Stegosaurus* (see page 27) and had a different arrangement of spikes and plates. It also had two large spikes sticking out sideways from its shoulders, which made formidable defensive weapons against predators such as *Ceratosaurus* (see page 13). *Kentrosaurus* means "spiky lizard."

Kentrosaurus lived **155–150 million years**. Fossil remains have been found in Tanzania, Africa. It grew up to 16.4 feet (5 m) long and weighed around 2.2 tons (2 tonnes).

MAMENCHISAURUS

This amazing **sauropod** had the longest neck for its body size of any dinosaur — measuring 29.5 feet (9 m), its neck was almost half its total body length. Like all **sauropods**, *Mamenchisaurus* was a plant eater. Its spoon-shaped teeth were used like a rake to strip leaves off plants. It swallowed leaves whole, without chewing them, and may have had to eat gastroliths (stomach stones) to help it digest the tough plant material. Its name means "Mamenchi lizard."

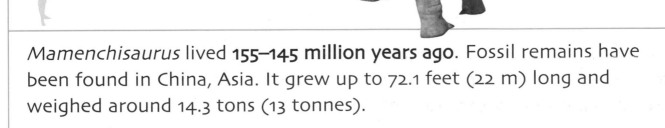

Mamenchisaurus lived **155–145 million years ago**. Fossil remains have been found in China, Asia. It grew up to 72.1 feet (22 m) long and weighed around 14.3 tons (13 tonnes).

MIRAGAIA

Miragaia, named after the area where it was found in Portugal, Europe, was a herbivorous **stegosaur**. These large quadrupeds usually fed on low-lying vegetation, but this particular **stegosaur** had an elongated neck with 17 vertebrae! This extra reach allowed it to browse for plants higher up. Like all **stegosaurs**, *Miragaia* had large plates running down its back in pairs, and a vicious four-spike thagomizer. It also had two large shoulder spikes.

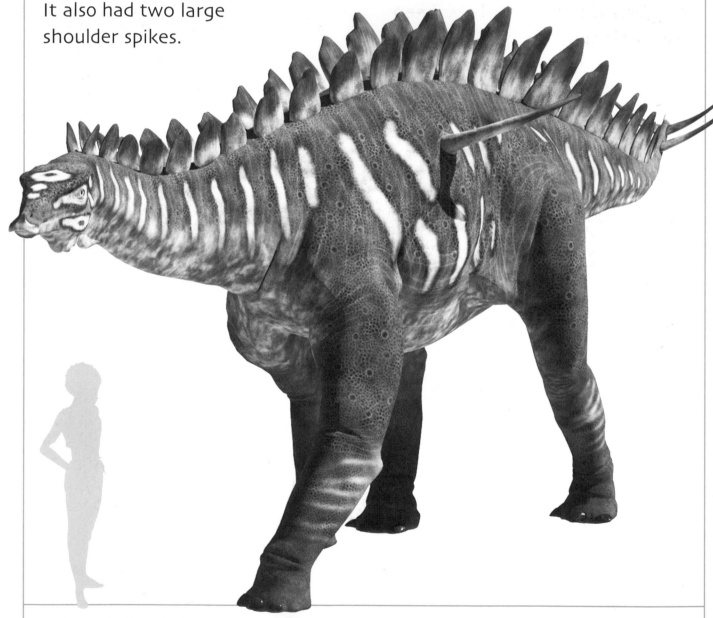

Miragaia lived about **150 million years ago**. Its fossil remains were found at a village called Miragaia in Portugal, Europe. It grew to 18 to 20 feet (5.5–6 m) long and weighed around 2.2 tons (2 tonnes).

ORNITHOLESTES

Ornitholestes, meaning "bird robber," was a small, lightly built **theropod** dinosaur. It was light on its feet and had a long tail that helped it balance as it ran on its two hind legs. It had strong arms with clawed hands that were ideal for capturing prey such as lizards and small mammals. *Ornitholestes* was probably covered in downy feathers, which suggests that it might have been warm blooded.

Ornitholestes lived **154–150 million years ago**. Fossil remains have been found in the United States, North America. It grew up to 6.6 feet (2 m) long and weighed around 33 pounds (15 kg).

SAUROPHAGANAX

Saurophaganax, meaning "lizard eater," was one of the largest **carnosaurs** of the Upper Jurassic. It was similar to *Allosaurus* (see page 6) but much bigger. It preyed on plant-eating dinosaurs such as *Camptosaurus* (see page 12), *Dryosaurus* and *Stegosaurus*. It may have attacked juvenile **sauropods,** too, such as *Camarasaurus* (see page 11) and *Diplodocus* (see page 17).

Saurophaganax lived around **150 million years ago**. Fossil remains have been found in the United States, North America. It grew up to 42 feet (12.8 m) long and weighed around 3 tons (2.7 tonnes).

STEGOSAURUS

Stegosaurus means "roof lizard." So-called because of its bony plates, it was a **stegosaur** dinosaur. Its plates might have been used to regulate its body temperature. The spikes at the end of its tail formed a thagomizer that was probably used as a defensive weapon.

Stegosaurus lived **155–145 million years ago**. Fossil remains have been found in Portugal, Europe, and in the United States, North America. It grew up to 29.5 feet (9 m) long and weighed around 5 tons (4.5 tonnes).

SUPERSAURUS

Supersaurus, meaning "super lizard," was a giant **diplodocid sauropod**. It was similar to *Apatosaurus* (see page 7) but had a more graceful build. The bones in its neck were longer than those of *Apatosaurus* and gave this **sauropod** one of the longest necks of any dinosaur. This would have allowed it to reach the succulent horsetails, club mosses and ferns that grew in the soft, marsh ground where the heavier giants could not go.

Supersaurus lived around **153 million years ago**. Fossil remains have been found in the United States, North America, and in Portugal, Europe. It grew up to 112 feet (34 m) long and weighed around 35 tons (31 tonnes).

TORVOSAURUS

Torvosaurus means "savage lizard." It was a very large, carnivorous **theropod** also known as a **megalosaur**. It had a long skull with powerful jaws filled with blade-like teeth, which were much thicker and stronger than those of *Allosaurus* (see page 6). *Torvosaurus* had powerful front arms with enlarged thumb claws. It could take down big herbivores such as *Stegosaurus* (see page 27) and *Miragaia* (see page 24), as well as **sauropods** like *Diplodocus* (see page 17).

Torvosaurus lived about **145 million years ago**. Fossil remains have been found in the United States, North America, and in Portugal, Europe. It grew between 33 and 40 feet (10–12 m) in length and weighed 4.4 to 5.5 tons (3.9–4.9 tonnes).

YANGCHUANOSAURUS

Yangchuanosaurus was a large, meat-eating **theropod**. It is named "lizard from Yangchuan" because its fossils were discovered in Yangchuan, in China, Asia. It had a large head with powerful jaws and a long tail that made up half its length. It preyed upon large **sauropods** such as *Mamenchisaurus* (see page 23) and *Omeisaurus*, as well as the stegosaurids *Chialingosaurus*, *Tuojiangosaurus* and *Chungkingosaurus*.

Yangchuanosaurus lived around **155–145 million years ago**. Fossil remains have been found in China. It grew to an estimated 26.2 feet (8 m) long and weighed around 2.2 to 3.3 tons (2–3 tonnes).

GLOSSARY

ankylosaur
A family of bulky quadrupedal, armored dinosaurs that had a club-like tail. The family included *Ankylosaurus* and *Euoplocephalus*.

carnosaur
A member of a group of large predatory dinosaurs, encompassing all the allosaurs.

diplodocid
A member of the sauropods, which had some of the longest creatures that ever walked the Earth. This group included *Diplodocus* and *Supersaurus*.

dromaeosaur
A family of bird-like theropod dinosaurs with a large, curved claw on the second toe, which included the famous *Velociraptor*.

megalosaur
A group of fairly primitive, stiff-tailed, carnivorous theropod dinosaurs, with razor-sharp teeth and three claws on each hand. This group included *Megalosaurus* and *Torvosaurus*.

ornithopod
A group of "bird-hipped" dinosaurs, characterized by being fast-paced grazers. It became one of the most successful herbivore groups.

pterosaur
Flying reptiles that included *Pterodactylus*.

sauropod
A group of large, four-legged, herbivorous dinosaurs with long necks and long tails. This group included the well-known *Brachiosaurus*, *Diplodocus* and *Apatosaurus*.

stegosaur
A member of a group of quadrupedal herbivores, characterized by their bony plates and, occasionally, a thagomizer. The family included *Miragaia* and the renowned *Stegosaurus*.

theropod
The large group of lizard-hipped dinosaurs that walked on two legs and included most of the giant carnivores such as *Tyrannosaurus*.

troodon
A group of bird-like theropod dinosaurs.